A TRUE BOOK™

P9-DUE-149

The Rhode Island Colony

KEVIN CUNNINGHAM

Children's Press®
An Imprint of Scholastic Inc.
New York Toronto London Auckland Sydney
Mexico City New Delhi Hong Kong
Danbury, Connecticut

Content Consultant
Jeffrey Kaja, PhD
Associate Professor of History
California State University, Northridge

Library of Congress Cataloging-in-Publication Data

Cunningham, Kevin, 1966–
  The Rhode Island Colony/Kevin Cunningham.
     p. cm.—(A true book)
  Includes bibliographical references and index.
  ISBN-13: 978-0-531-25397-7 (lib. bdg.)   ISBN-13: 978-0-531-26610-6 (pbk.)
  ISBN-10: 0-531-25397-X (lib. bdg.)   ISBN-10: 0-531-26610-9 (pbk.)
  1. Rhode Island—History—Colonial period, ca. 1600–1775—Juvenile
literature. I. Title.
  F82.C86 2011
  974.5'02—dc22   2011009634

All rights reserved. Published in 2012 by Children's Press, an imprint of Scholastic Inc.
Printed in China 62
SCHOLASTIC, CHILDREN'S PRESS, A TRUE BOOK, and associated logos are trademarks and/or registered trademarks of Scholastic Inc.
1 2 3 4 5 6 7 8 9 10 R 21 20 19 18 17 16 15 14 13 12

Find the Truth!

Everything you are about to read is true *except* for one of the sentences on this page.

Which one is **TRUE**?

T or F   Rhode Island played a large role in the slave trade.

T or F   Taxes had nothing to do with Rhode Island seeking independence.

Find the answers in this book.

Contents

A husking bee

Nathanael Greene

5 A War for Independence

THE **BIG** TRUTH!

Rhode Island's Founding Fathers

Colonial "dame schools" were based on similar schools in 16th-century England.

Timeline of Rhode Island Colony History

Around 8,000 years ago

Native Americans settle Rhode Island and the surrounding areas.

1636

Roger Williams starts the colony of Providence.

1647

The General Assembly of Providence Plantations is formed.

1772

Protesters set fire to the British ship *Gaspee*.

1790

Rhode Island becomes a state.

First Nation

Early Native American groups settled in Rhode Island thousands of years before it was colonized by Europeans. These groups developed into peoples such as the Narragansett, the Pequot, and the Wampanoag. About 7,000 Narragansett lived in the region in 1600. They were the most powerful native group residing there. Their main villages were on the shores or islands of Narragansett Bay. A chief called a sachem was the leader of each village. The Pequot peoples lived to the west. The Wampanoag lived to the east.

Men at Work

Narragansett men hunted deer, turkey, and beaver with bows and arrows. At the ocean shore they dug oysters and clams out of tide pools. They rowed dugout canoes made of hollowed-out tree trunks to catch fish and eels. Males also had the responsibility of growing tobacco. The Narragansett believed the leafy plant cured headaches and arthritis.

Native Americans acquired much of their food through fishing.

Wigwams were used by several native groups in the Northeast.

Village Women

The Narragansett surrounded their summer villages with fields of maize (corn), squash, and beans. The women tended these small farms. Women and children added to the food supply by gathering berries and other wild plants. Women also made clothing from animal skins and furs. As winter approached, women took down the family's wigwam, a type of movable house. The family moved to a village away from the stormy seashore and built the wigwam again.

Area
enlarged

Original
13 Colonies

Blackstone River

NIPMUC

Cumberland •

MASSACHUSETTS

CONNECTICUT

Providence •

RHODE
ISLAND

Warren •

Bristol •

Greenwich •

N A R R A G A N S E T T

Narragansett Bay

Portsmouth •

*Rhode
Island*

Newport •

MOHEGAN

Kingstown •

□ Fort
George

Pawcatuck River

ATLANTIC OCEAN

━━━ Colonial boundaries

*Block
Island*

0 ——— miles ——— 10
0 —— km —— 10

CHAPTER 2

Settlers From Far Away

Local Native Americans met Italian explorer Giovanni da Verrazano when he sailed into Narragansett Bay in 1524. But it wasn't until the 1600s that native peoples had steady contact with Europeans. Dutch traders lived in forts to the west. They traded polished shell beads called wampum to Native Americans for beaver and otter furs. The Narragansett lacked metalworking abilities. They traded for Dutch knives, axes, and other tools.

Williams served as a peacemaker and translator between the Narragansett and colonists.

Roger Williams

Europeans began to settle on the coast of present-day Massachusetts in the 1620s. Religious thinker Roger Williams was exiled, or forced out, from England's Massachusetts Bay **Colony** in 1636. Williams had spoken out harshly against the Church of England. He also preached the unpopular ideas of religious freedom and fair treatment of Native Americans. Williams used a gift of land from two Narragansett sachems to start his own colony.

Twelve families joined Williams to found the town of Providence in modern-day Rhode Island. Williams treated his Native American neighbors with respect. He made honest deals with them and learned their languages. He also granted his settlers religious freedom. He encouraged them to speak at town meetings. Rhode Island had four towns by 1642. Each had its own laws. The towns joined together into a single colony when Massachusetts and Connecticut threatened to take their land.

Colonists arrive at the new Providence settlement.

Providence Plantations

Williams obtained a **charter** from England's King Charles I in 1644. It stated that the colony was independent from others. The colony was named Providence Plantations. It formed a General Assembly to make laws. Religious groups fleeing **prejudice** in England and other colonies came to Providence. Growing and selling crops such as maize and tobacco replaced the fur trade as a way to make a living. The population of the colony reached 1,200 people in 1655.

Land had to be cleared of trees before it could be farmed.

Newport was founded in 1639.

A New Charter

A new charter was granted in 1663 to help the colony once again resist its land-grabbing neighbors. The charter changed the colony's name to Rhode Island. It also allowed Rhode Islanders to elect their own governor. This was an unusual freedom in any American colony at that time. The General Assembly set up headquarters in Newport. Newport was a growing port city with a booming **economy** built on shipping, whaling, and trading.

War With the Narragansett

Massachusetts's native peoples went to war in 1675 to take back land claimed by settlers. The Narragansett refused to join the conflict at first. But in December, armed settlers from outside Rhode Island attacked and killed hundreds of Narragansett in December. The Narragansett burned Providence and Warwick in spring 1676. The colonists responded by killing the Narragansett head sachem. Many Native Americans left Rhode Island when the war ended in August.

Colonists launch an attack against a Narragansett village.

By 1774, a third of British merchant ships were built in American colonies.

A Threat From England

King James II forced the colony to join with the rest of New England under a single government in 1685. The experiment ended three years later. King William III assumed the throne. Rhode Island was again permitted to choose its own government. The colony thrived. Newport silver and iron goods became famous throughout the colonies. So did candles and ships made in Rhode Island. But much of the colony's success relied on less respectable businesses.

Native Americans were occasionally sold as slaves.

Smugglers brought goods into Rhode Island without paying taxes on their cargo. This was a serious crime. Newport also hosted dozens of **privateers**. These pirates were hired by England to harass enemies such as France and Spain. Newport businessmen began to sell African slaves in 1696. Many **merchants** became wealthy in the slave trade. This allowed them to build large houses and buy stylish clothing.

Anne Hutchinson

Anne Hutchinson was thrown out of the Massachusetts Bay Colony for her unpopular ideas. She studied the Bible on her own. Her interpretations often conflicted with Puritan teachings. Hutchinson and around 80 followers joined Roger Williams about two years after he settled Providence. The Narragansett gave Hutchinson's group land on Aquidneck Island. The group founded Portsmouth in 1638. Hutchinson went to New York after her husband died. She was killed by Native Americans in 1643.

CHAPTER 3

Life in Rhode Island

Children in Rhode Island often led difficult lives. As many as four in 10 died before reaching adulthood during the 1600s. Children spent most of their time doing chores. Farm children milked cows and chopped firewood. Boys living in town often worked with their fathers at the family business. Girls helped their mothers take care of the household.

Colonial women did most of their cooking in or around a large fireplace.

Boys were more likely to attend school than girls were.

Colonial children attend a dame school in the teacher's home.

Schooling

Rhode Island children learned reading and writing at home. Only a few towns opened schools. Some women ran "dame schools" from their homes. These were a type of private elementary school. Few children had a higher education. Many boys left home to serve as **apprentices**. An apprentice spent a number of years with a tradesman who taught him a special skill such as carpentry or metalworking.

Women at Work

Most women spent their days taking care of their children and cooking. They sewed clothes, spun wool, and kept gardens. Many farm women earned money by making and selling items such as yarn, butter, or medicine. Time with friends was spent at church and social events. Farm families met to husk corn at husking bees. Then they feasted, danced, and played music.

Colonists used husking bees as a chance to get together with others in the community.

Colonial Rhode Island farmers commonly raised sheep, apples, onions, and dairy products.

PLOUGH DEEP WHILE SLUGGARDS SLEEP; AND YOU SHALL HAVE CORN TO SELL AND TO KE...

WORK TODAY FOR YOU KNOW NOT HOW MUCH YOU MAY BE HINDERED TOMORROW.

Earning a Living

Farmers and their older sons plowed and planted the field. They took the crops to sell at local markets. The work started before sunrise and often ended after sunset. Owners of large farms, called plantations, hired other people or bought African slaves to grow the crops. More men went into trades and other businesses as time passed.

24

Slaves

Enslaved people had no rights or freedoms. Owners could beat them or sell their family members. Children of slaves were born slaves. Rhode Island merchants played a major role

Slaves had no choices regarding how they lived or worked.

in American slavery. They organized hundreds of slaving trips to Africa to capture slaves. According to some historians, more than 100,000 slaves passed through Newport and other cities before 1774. Rhode Island made it illegal to bring new slaves into the colony that year.

Rhode Island's population included a Jewish community, which fled to the colony from Barbados in 1658 for religious freedom.

CHAPTER 4

Taxes and Trouble

Rhode Island's powerful economy drew settlers from England and from other colonies. About 59,000 people lived in Rhode Island by 1774. Many towns such as Bristol and Cumberland joined Rhode Island from the 1720s to the 1740s. But trouble with Britain threatened Rhode Island's success as the 1700s continued.

Jewish colonists completed the Touro Synagogue in 1763 in Newport.

Britain and its Native American allies fought France and its Native American allies for control of North America from 1754 to 1763. The conflict was called the French and Indian War. Britain won the war. But it had to borrow large amounts of money to pay for the war and to protect the western edge of the American colonies. Parliament, the British **legislature**, decided to raise money by taxing certain products in the colonies.

American colonists fought alongside British troops in the French and Indian War.

Both British taxes and colonial protests affected what merchants were able to buy and sell in the colonies.

A tax was put on sugar and molasses. Newport used large amounts of molasses to make a drink called rum. They sold the rum in the colonies and overseas. Merchants complained about the tax. But few made trouble over it. Emotions began to run high when Parliament imposed the Stamp Act of 1765. This new tax forced colonists to buy a stamp to put on printed matter such as newspapers and legal documents.

"Taxation Without Representation"

The colonists protested the Stamp Act even before it took effect. But colonists did not oppose all taxes. Most people paid taxes to colonial governments. But the colonists elected the representatives to those governments. No colony could elect representatives to Parliament. The colonists had no one to argue for a colony's rights. They began to complain about "taxation without representation."

People all across the colonies protested British taxes.

Parliament withdrew the Stamp Act in early 1766. But Parliament imposed more taxes over the next few years. The colonists' anger and resistance grew. People in Newport set the British ship *Liberty* on fire in 1769. A ship named the *Gaspee* met the same fate in 1772. Some Rhode Islanders joined an anti-British group called the Sons of Liberty that had members throughout the colonies.

The *Gaspee's* crew was taken prisoner and sent ashore before colonists burned the ship.

CHAPTER 5

A War for Independence

The British government sent more ships and soldiers to Newport to control the colonists. This angered Rhode Islanders opposed to British rule. Other colonists approved of Britain's actions. They were called Loyalists. Colonists and Britain soon clashed over a tax on tea. Parliament also allowed a British company to sell its tea tax-free. American companies still had to pay a tax.

 Colonists sometimes had to allow British soldiers to stay in their homes.

Tea Parties

Members of the Sons of Liberty dumped a shipload of British tea into Boston Harbor in December 1773. The event became known as the Boston Tea Party. On March 2, 1775, people in Providence held a tea party of their own by burning tea in a large fire in the center of town. Storekeepers added to the protest by refusing to sell British tea. The British and American colonists had reached a boiling point.

Two of the ships boarded in the Boston Tea Party were owned by a Massachusetts colonist.

British soldiers began raiding colonists' homes when food and other supplies became scarce.

The Revolutionary War Begins

On April 19, 1775, British troops and American **militia** fought at Lexington and Concord in Massachusetts. The American Revolutionary War had begun. Soldiers from both sides moved toward nearby Boston. But Rhode Island's Loyalist governor refused to let Rhode Island's militia join the colonial forces. Britain's navy quickly blocked Newport Harbor. British soldiers raided local farms for food, animals, and other supplies. A British force occupied Newport on December 8, 1776.

Rhode Island's Founding Fathers

Representatives from 12 of the 13 colonies met at the First Continental Congress in Philadelphia in 1774. The Congress's request for respect and fairer treatment from King George III failed. A second Congress met in May 1775 to decide its next course of action. The Congress created a Continental army and made George Washington its commander in chief. The representatives began to discuss becoming independent from Britain in the spring of 1776. Rhode Island declared independence on May 4. The Congress voted two months later to approve the Declaration of Independence.

Stephen Hopkins

Stephen Hopkins was elected governor of Rhode Island nine times. He had spoken out against British control as early as 1764. He helped organize the American navy during the war. Hopkins was one of the colony's two signers of the declaration.

Samuel Ward

Samuel Ward was another former governor. He was known for his refusal to obey the Stamp Act in 1765. Ward was a member of the Second Continental Congress. But he died in spring 1776 before he could cast a vote for independence. Ellery took his place at the Congress.

William Ellery

William Ellery was a Newport native. He practiced law and belonged to the Sons of Liberty. Ellery joined the Second Continental Congress after Samuel Ward died. He was one of the colony's two signers of the declaration. He worked for the government after the war and joined the fight to eliminate slavery.

French troops fought against the British at the Battle of Rhode Island.

Battle of Rhode Island

The largest battle fought on Rhode Island soil occurred in 1778. The Second Continental Congress had ordered Rhode Islanders to raise an army. They were unable to find enough men. The state offered enslaved people their freedom in return for serving. About 250 men accepted. General John Sullivan and Nathanael Greene commanded white and black troops at the Battle of Rhode Island in August. But Continental forces failed to push the British out of Newport.

Nathanael Greene

Nathanael Greene was Rhode Island's most famous Revolutionary War hero. He led troops in many early battles. He was one of George Washington's most trusted generals. Washington chose Greene to lead the Continental army in the south after the Battle of Rhode Island. Greene wore out the British armies in the Carolinas and Georgia through a series of chases and battles. Grateful Georgians gave him land to settle on after the war.

While Americans celebrated their victory in the Revolutionary War, they also faced the difficult task of rebuilding.

After the War

Britain's main forces surrendered after losing a battle at Yorktown, Virginia, in October 1781. The American victory came at a high cost. Thousands were killed or wounded. The colonies had gone into debt to pay for the war. British ships that blocked trade into American ports had ruined many businesses. Towns and farms had been damaged. The British had burned dozens of buildings in Newport. They also destroyed the wharves the city used for shipping.

The Constitution

Americans had to answer an important question after the war. Did the new country need a strong national government? Those who said yes believed it was the only way to bring the states together into one nation. Those who said no worried that a powerful government would treat them unfairly. Representatives from 12 states met in Philadelphia in 1787 to decide on a **constitution** that would create a new American government.

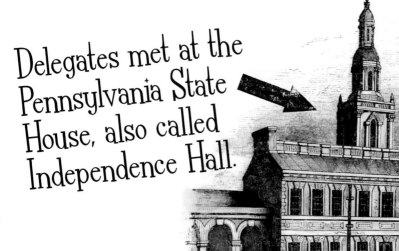

Delegates met at the Pennsylvania State House, also called Independence Hall.

Rhode Island refused to attend the meeting. Residents of the state felt that the nation did not need the new constitution. Rhode Islanders opposed the new U.S. Constitution when it went to each state for approval. Even the passage of the Bill of Rights, guaranteeing freedom of religion and speech, could not change their vote. But Providence threatened to break away from Rhode Island unless the Rhode Island representatives approved the U.S. Constitution. Rhode Island finally approved it on May 29, 1790. It was the last of the 13 colonies to accept the document. ★

Rhode Island's state flag was officially adopted in 1879.

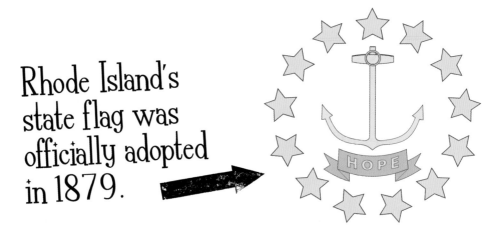

True Statistics

Number of Narragansett in 1600: About 7,000

Number of families who joined Roger Williams: 12

Number of Rhode Island towns in 1642: 4

Number of Rhode Island settlers in 1655: 1,200

Time an apprentice worked for a tradesman: 5 to 6 years

Number of slaves that may have passed through Newport: More than 100,000

Population of Rhode Island in 1774: About 59,000

Amount of time British troops occupied Newport: 3 years

Number of slaves who fought for Rhode Island in 1778: About 250

Year Britain surrendered in Revolutionary War: 1781

Did you find the truth?

T Rhode Island played a large role in the slave trade.

F Taxes had nothing to do with Rhode Island seeking independence.

Resources

Books

Hallinan, Val. *Rhode Island*. New York: Children's Press, 2009.

Italia, Bob. *The Rhode Island Colony*. Edina, MN: Checkerboard, 2001.

Jensen, Niels R. *Rhode Island*. Edina, MN: ABDO, 2010.

Koontz, Robin. *Rhode Island: The Ocean State*. New York: PowerKids Press, 2011.

Landau, Elaine. *The Declaration of Independence*. New York: Children's Press, 2008.

Marsh, Carole. *Rhode Island Native Americans*. Peachtree City, GA: Gallopade International, 2004.

Raum, Elizabeth. *Roger Williams*. Chicago: Heinemann-Raintree, 2005.

Thoennes Keller, Kristin. *The Slave Trade in Early America*. Mankato, MN: Capstone, 2004.

Organizations and Web Sites

Narragansett Indian Tribe

www.narragansett-tribe.org
Learn about Narragansett history and find out what is happening in the Narragansett community today.

Rhode Island Historical Society

www.rihs.org
Find out facts about Rhode Island from one of the country's oldest historical societies.

Places to Visit

Museum of Newport History

127 Thames Street
Newport, RI 02840
(401) 841-8770
www.newporthistorical.org
/index.php/museum-shop
/museum-of-newport-history
Study exhibits that tell the story of one of Rhode Island's oldest and most important cities.

South County Museum

100 Strathmore Street
Narragansett, RI 02882
(401) 783-5400
www.southcountymuseum.org
Visit this living museum to see how Rhode Islanders lived and worked in the past.

Important Words

apprentices (uh-PREN-tis-ez) — people who learn a skill by working with an expert

charter (CHAHR-tur) — a formal document guaranteeing rights or privileges

colony (KAH-luh-nee) — an area settled by people from another country and controlled by that country

constitution (kahn-sti-TOO-shun) — the laws of a country that state the rights of the people and the powers of government

economy (ih-KA-ne-mee) — the system of buying, selling, and making things and managing money

legislature (LEJ-is-lay-chur) — a group of people who have the power to make or change laws

merchants (MUR-chuhntz) — people who buy and sell goods to make money

militia (muh-LISH-uh) — a group of people who are trained to fight but who aren't professional soldiers

prejudice (PREJ-uh-dis) — unreasonable or unfair opinion based on a person's religion, race, or other characteristic

privateers (prye-ve-TEERZ) — armed men given permission by a government to raid enemy ships and territory

smugglers (SMUHG-luhrz) — people who bring goods into or out of a country illegally

Index

Page numbers in **bold** indicate illustrations

About the Author

Kevin Cunningham has written more than 40 books on disasters, the history of disease, Native Americans, and other topics. Cunningham lives near Chicago with his wife and young daughter.